Xtreme Athletes
Kelly Slater

Kelly Slater

Jeff C. Young

PUBLISHING

Greensboro, North Carolina

Xtreme Athletes

Michael Phelps
David Beckham
Danica Patrick
Kelly Slater
Shaun White

XTREME ATHLETES: KELLY SLATER

Copyright © 2009 by Jeff C. Young

Library of Congress Cataloging-in-Publication Data

Young, Jeff C., 1948-
  Xtreme athletes : Kelly Slater / by Jeff C. Young.
    p. cm.
  Includes bibliographical references and index.
  ISBN 978-1-59935-078-3
  1. Slater, Kelly, 1972--Juvenile literature. 2. Surfers--United States--
Biography--Juvenile literature. I. Title.
  GV838.S53Y68 2007
  797.3'2092--dc22
  [B]

                                              2007042943

Printed in the United States of America

First Edition

To Duke Kahanamoku and his boys, for showing the world how to go surfing

Contents

Kelly Slater
(Courtesy of RAFA RIVAS/AFP/Getty Images)

one

Paddling Out

Kelly Slater was born near the ocean. In the east Florida town of Cocoa Beach, where he was born on February 11, 1972, he learned to surf.

"It was a great place to start," he said. "It gave my surfing a good foundation. The waves were slow and user-friendly. I could figure out my moves in slow motion before trying them out at full speed."

Kelly's parents loved spending time at the beach. His father, Steve, was a surfer and lifeguard, and he owned a bait and tackle store on the beach. His mother, Judy, regularly took Kelly and his older brother, Sean, for long visits to the beach.

Kelly's hometown of Cocoa Beach, Florida

When he was five years old, Kelly began surfing with his brother Sean, as a way to pass the time during those long trips to the beach. "I think that it was out of boredom that Sean and I began riding waves," he said.

He started out surfing on a cheap Styrofoam bellyboard. The board was flimsy and frail, but it was good enough for someone who was just learning to surf. During the winter months when the water temperature dipped into the low sixties, Sean and Kelly donned their wetsuits and continued to surf. When there weren't any waves big enough to ride, they rode a homemade, simulation surfboard in their back yard, rigging up a device called a surf swing, for which the brothers used a rope to tie a piece of plywood to a big tree branch. Kelly also honed his surfing skills by riding a skateboard, helping with balance and poise.

After using a bellyboard for about a year, Kelly moved up to using a bodyboard. On a bodyboard, the user lies on his stomach instead of standing up like you do on a surfboard. That wasn't for Kelly, though: "I wanted to surf, so I rode it standing up, making balance a little more difficult. Since I had already been standing up on my Styrofoam plug, my bodyboard was a step up."

At the age of eight, Kelly entered and won his first surfing competition. In surfing competitions a series of heats with two to four surfers competing are observed by a panel of judges scoring each ride on a scale of one to ten. Then, each surfer's top two scores are combined for a total heat score. The victory goes to the surfer who performs "radical controlled maneuvers in the critical section of the wave with speed, power, and flow." The scoring system has been likened to a gymnastics meet with elements of intimidation and showmanship thrown in.

Still riding the bodyboard, Kelly pestered his father to buy him a real surfboard. His dad gave in, but Kelly had to wait over six months for his board to be custom-built: at the time, no one stocked surfboards built and designed just for kids.

When he was nine, Kelly used his new board to compete in the Eastern Surfing Association's (ESA) Championships at Cape Hatteras, North Carolina. It was his first competition outside of Florida, and Kelly was awed by the size and intensity of the waves. He finished last in the twelve-and-under division.

At that time, Kelly was finding he had more to worry about than working up the courage to challenge big, fast waves. His father's persistent drinking was causing problems. Although his father

Cape Hatteras, North Carolina *(Courtesy of the U.S. Air Force)*

wasn't physically abusive, Kelly witnessed yelling and arguing between his parents. Kelly's mother wanted his father out of the house, but Kelly kept convincing her to let him stay.

The turning point in Kelly's relationship with his father came during the 1982 ESA Championships in Cape Hatteras. No longer intimidated by the big

Kelly with his mom, Judy, in 2006. *(Courtesy of Pierre Tostee/ASP/Getty Images)*

waves off of the North Carolina coast, Kelly won the twelve-and-under division. But at a post-tournament party, his dad started drinking. Kelly and Sean urged their father to leave and drive them back to Cocoa Beach, but their father started yelling at his sons like he would yell at his wife.

"It was the first and only time that he ever became belligerent with me," Kelly recalled, "and my life came to a screeching halt. . . . The next time that my mom told me that she wanted my dad to leave, I decided I would be right behind her."

Upon falling out with his father, Kelly focused even more on his surfing. "Surfing was the one thing that was always there for me," he said. "It made me smile . . . As long as I continued to improve and win contests, our problems at home couldn't touch me."

Kelly, seeing the damage alcohol had done to his father and family, decided he had no interest in drugs or alcohol. He became dismayed when he found that some of the local surfers that he had looked up to were also drug users. "I never could see the good in getting stoned," he said. "Soon word spread that I was serious about not doing drugs. . . . As I got older, I chose friends who felt the same way about drugs as I did. Surfing is my high."

In 1983, Kelly's parents split up, and his father left home. He refused to give up drinking, though he still drove Kelly and Sean all around Florida to compete in surfing contests. But his absence put a financial strain on the family. Kelly's mother could no longer make the mortgage payments on their house, and they lived in a succession of low-rent condos.

Kelly was regularly competing and winning in amateur contests, but that wasn't bringing in any money to help out the family. Fortunately, he soon found a sponsor to help out with travel expenses and provide some income.

A surfboard manufacturer, Sundek, introduced a line of Sean and Kelly Slater signature model surfboards. While the boards were being made and sold, they gave Sean cash payments of $120 a week and Kelly $105. Though Kelly later admitted he never cared for Sundek's boards, he greatly appreciated the steady income the sponsorship provided for his struggling family.

Furthermore, Sundek gave Kelly the means to compete in tournaments in Puerto Rico and

Barbados while he was still in high school. It gave him the chance to face tougher competition and ride bigger waves, a vital learning experience. "These experiences were just the gentle nudge that I needed to get comfortable," he said. "They added to my surfing knowledge and gave me a feel for size and power, since bigger waves move faster and with more force."

Still, things were not always easy for Kelly, and his relationship with his brother was being tested. Sean and Kelly had always had a natural sibling rivalry. They both had local Cocoa Beach surfer Matt Kechele as their mentor, but Kelly had become the star pupil. Sean was three years older than Kelly and it irked him to see his younger brother winning more trophies and contests and getting more attention. Kelly explained:

> Deep down, [Sean] was my biggest supporter, but it didn't always come out that way . . . there were times when he flat out said that he hated me. We each wanted the same things out of surfing, but I was the one getting pictures in magazines and all the attention. The better I did, the harder it was for Sean, and it started to make us drift apart.

The beach at South Padre Island, Texas, where the 1988 World Amateur Championships were held

Regardless of how Sean felt, Kelly was regularly beating older, more experienced surfers. By the time he was sixteen, he had won six East Coast surfing titles, four U.S. Championships and two NSSA Nationals.

But while Kelly was being hailed by surfing magazines as a teenage phenom and a future world champion, he suffered the biggest setback of his young career. In November 1987, the team trials for the picking the U.S. Team for the 1988 World Amateur Championships were held in South Padre Island, Texas; Kelly failed to make the team. He was offered the position of second alternate, but turned it down.

"As competitive as I was, there was no way that I could sit on the sidelines and watch the event. I couldn't stand losing in anything I tried, especially surfing."

Win or lose, surfing had become Kelly's life. Traveling to tourneys was causing him to miss classes at Cocoa Beach High School, but he was so disciplined and focused his grades didn't suffer. During his last two years of high school, he completed all of his homework and assignments during study hall. Even when he was out of school competing in surfing tournaments, he kept up with his classes.

When he graduated in 1991, Kelly had a 3.4 grade point average and ranked seventh in his class of 130. Although he had turned pro in July 1990, he felt it was important to at least finish high school.

"If you can't finish high school, there probably aren't a lot of things in life that you can finish," he said.

Once he was handed his high school diploma, Kelly was ready to totally dedicate himself to surfing. He no longer had the distraction of being a full-time student and part-time surfer. Over the next seven years, Slater would come to dominate his sport like Lance Armstrong in cycling or Tiger Woods in golf.

two
History of the Surf

It's not known exactly where and when surfing began. There is a general agreement that the sport was first practiced in Polynesia, a group of scattered islands in the central and south Pacific Ocean. It's generally believed that it began sometime before 1000 A.D.

The British explorer James Cook is credited with being the first European to report surfing to the rest of the world. During his voyages to Hawaii, Cook wrote in his journals about seeing men and women on boards, riding waves.

Captain James Cook

The first documented instances of surfing appeared in the journals of English explorer Captain James Cook. Born in 1728, Cook was the son of Scottish farm laborer. Initially apprenticed at a haberdashery, Cook found that a retailer's life was not for him; he was drawn to the sea. He became an apprentice on a merchant ship, and spent the next several years serving on a variety of ships, before joining the British Royal Navy in 1755.

After serving in the Seven Years War, Cook advanced to the rank of commander, and was hired by the Royal Society of London for the Improvement of Natural Knowledge to explore foreign oceans for scientific observation. Sailing for the Royal Society, Cook was the first Englishman to land on the Eastern shore of Australia, and circumnavigate New Zealand. He also mapped Newfoundland, and drew up carefully detailed maps of his voyages. He published the journals of his voyages, making him a minor celebrity in the scientific community for his careful observation of natural phenomena.

It was on his third and final voyage of exploration, begun in 1776 that Cook came to Hawaii. He was the first European to visit the islands in 1778, where he observed local natives riding on the waves atop giant wooden boards, which he carefully described in his journal. He named the Hawaiian archipelago the Sandwich Islands after John Montagu, the

fourth Earl of Sandwich, who was one of the sponsors of his expedition.

From Hawaii, Cook sailed north, toward the Bering Strait, all the way up to Alaska, where the Cook Inlet was named for him. However, his attempts to sail through the Bering Strait failed, and in 1779, he returned to Hawaii.

Some historians speculate that Cook carefully timed his return to Hawaii to coincide with a native religious festival for the Polynesian god Lono. Cook was aware that aspects of his ship, the HMS *Resolution* (particularly the mast and rigging), resembled images in the Polynesian religion associated with Lono, and that Cook took advantage of this to get the natives to welcome him as a deity.

Regardless of whether or not this was true, Cook and his crew spent about a month in Hawaii, recovering from their harrowing attempts to cross the Bering Strait and repairing their ship. But on February 14, 1779, after the season of worship for Lono had ended, Cook and his men got into an altercation with the natives; after they took one of his small boats, Cook and his men responded by taking several natives hostage, including a chief. In the ensuing scuffle, Cook was hit on the head and stabbed to death.

Cook's fellow captain, Charles Clerke, who accompanied him on the voyage, carried Cook's journals back to England, where they were completed and published by Captain James King. They gave the English an early view of the new world, and provided the first glimpse of surfing outside the native culture of Hawaii.

Author Mark Twain was one of the first Americans to write about surfing. While visiting Hawaii, Twain decided to give it a try. In his 1872 book, *Roughing It*, Twain writes:

In one place we came upon a large company of naked natives, of both sexes and all ages amusing themselves with the national pastime of surf-bathing. Each heathen would paddle three or four hundred yards out to sea (taking a short board with him), then face the shore and wait for a particularly prodigious billow to come along; at the right moment he would fling his board upon its foamy crest and himself upon the board and here he would come whizzing by like a bombshell! . . . I tried surf-bathing once, subsequently but made a failure of it. I got the board placed right and at the right moment, too; but missed the connection myself. The board struck the shore in

Mark Twain *(Courtesy of Library of Congress)*

three-quarters of a second without any cargo, and I struck the bottom at about the same time, with a couple of barrels of water in me. None but natives ever master the art of surf-bathing thoroughly.

By the late 1800s surfing in Hawaii had nearly ceased to exist. The native population was devastated by diseases brought in by foreign visitors; one estimate claims that only 10 percent of the native population survived in the years between the first outside contacts and the end of the nineteenth century. Furthermore, many of those outsiders were Christian missionaries, who discouraged pastimes like surfing as a waste of time.

Hawaiian islands

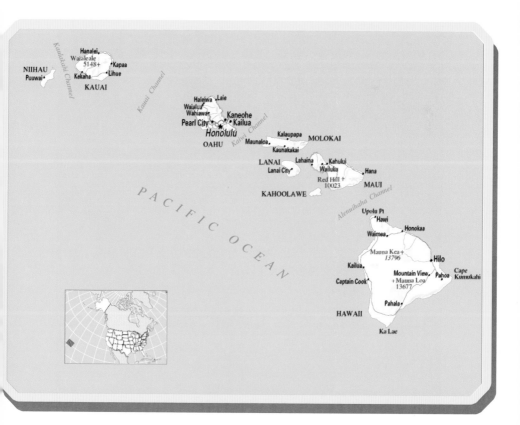

After Hawaii became a U.S. territory in 1900, the sport enjoyed a resurgence. A few surviving surfers congregated at Waikiki Beach and made a living introducing the sport to curious and adventurous tourists.

In the early twentieth century three surfing pioneers—Duke Kahanamoku, George Freeth, and

Duke Kahanamoku *(Courtesy of Library of Congress)*

Tom Blake—popularized surfing and helped it to spread to America and other parts of the world.

Kahanamoku first drew worldwide attention by winning a gold medal in the 100-meter freestyle swimming competition in the 1912 Olympics. Two years later he traveled to Australia and introduced surfing there in an exhibition at Freshwater Beach in Sydney. Later, he performed exhibitions in California, helping to make surfing a popular sport in America.

Freeth was considered by many of his peers to be the best surfer of his era. Born in Hawaii, Freeth was brought to Redondo Beach, California by the owners of the Redondo-Los Angeles Railway to entertain tourists and to promote the railroad.

They advertised Freeth as "The Man Who Can Walk on Water." Freeth would astound his audience by paddling out on his eight-foot, two-hundred pound solid wood surfboard and ride a wave onto the beach while standing upright. Freeth is also credited with being one of the first surfers to angle across a wave instead of riding it straight to the shoreline.

Freeth became better known for his work as a lifeguard: he was credited with saving at least seventy-eight people during his lifeguarding career. The stress and strain of performing strenuous rescue work eventually took its toll, though. He died at the age of thirty-five.

Tom Blake began surfing in 1924 while working as a lifeguard at the Santa Monica Swimming Club. He found an old surfboard that was being stored at the club and he taught himself to use it. Blake made frequent trips from California to Hawaii to surf. During one of his Hawaiian visits, Blake saw some ancient surfboards on display at the Bishop Museum in Honolulu. That inspired him to create lighter, more streamlined boards for both surfing and paddleboarding.

In the 1920s most surfboards weighed between ninety and 150 pounds. Because the boards were so heavy, surfing was an almost exclusively male sport. Blake was able to design and make sturdy boards that weighed forty to seventy pounds, allowing more women to enjoy the pleasures of surfing, and inspiring other surfers to design and manufacture lighter boards.

Boards became even lighter and more maneuverable with the advent of fiberglass. It enabled

Tom Blake created a lighter surfboard that enabled women to participate in the previously male-dominated sport of surfing. *(Courtesy of General Photographic Agency/Getty Images)*

Fiberglass surfboards like those seen here provided surfers with a lighter and more maneuverable way to surf.

builders to seal the board's soft balsa wood core with a lightweight material. Soon, all the heavier materials that had been used for sealing became obsolete. Boards became light enough for children and teens to use.

The Development of the Surfboard

As a modern surfer, Kelly Slater has largely spent his career surfing on fiberglass surfboards, about six to ten feet long, and between five to fifteen pounds. But surfboards in this style are a relatively contemporary development, as the surfboard has evolved dramatically over the last several hundred years.

The first surfboards—the ones documented by Captain Cook in the late eighteenth century—were solid boards, made from whatever wood grew locally. Called *papa he'e nalu* in the Hawaiian language, these boards were cumbersome, anywhere between ten and twenty feet in length, and usually weighing around seventy-seven pounds, but sometimes up to two hundred. As such, even getting these boards to the beach and into the ocean was an ordeal requiring great strength, and once in the water, the heavy boards were not especially buoyant.

Because these boards were simply solid pieces of wood, without any fins or shaping common to modern boards, riders were

unable to turn or do any kind of tricks. Waves were simply rode in a straight line toward the shore. Still, the sport of surfing was exhilarating enough that Hawaiian royalty practiced it on their own custom-made boards.

It was not until 1926 that the first known advancements were made on surfboards. It was then that Tom Blake built a hollow board. The hollow board was lighter and more buoyant than its solid wood counterpart, but it still lacked any shape that would allow surfers much control over their rides.

A surfer named Bob Simmons (1919-1954) took the first step towards making surfboards more maneuverable. He built a board called the Simmons Spoon, which had a slight curve from the nose (the front of the board) to the tail (the back). This curve, though slightly reducing speed, gave surfers more control over their movements. The curved shape has become customary in boards, and is now referred to as the rocker.

Meanwhile, Tom Blake further refined surfboards by attaching a fin to the board in 1935. The fin helped stabilize the board, preventing it from sliding sideways through the wave. The fin was further refined by a surfer named George Greenough in the 1960s. The champion Australian surfer Mark Richards added a second fin to his board, increasing his control, then another Australian surfer, Simon Anderson experimented with a third fin in the 1980s. In the 1990s, board manufacturers began offering boards with easily removable fins, not only making surfboards easier to transport, but also allowing surfers unprecedented customization of their boards.

Still, it was the development of fiberglass and polyurethanes that most revolutionized surfing. These synthetic materials allowed boards to be made that were smaller and more compact, and weighed considerably less. As such, the fiberglass boards were much more buoyant, and offered much more control to the surfer. This gave way to the style of trick-heavy performance surfing practiced by Slater and other contemporary surfers.

Though some surfers have attempted to bring back hollow wooden boards, and others have built custom boards out of carbon fiber and aluminum, the fiberglass and polyurethane boards remain the modern standard.

ANATOMY
of a
SURFBOARD

Nose
The tip of the surfboard.

Deck
The surface of the board, where the surfer stands.

Stringer
A thin piece of wood that runs from the nose to the tail, used to strengthen the board.

Rail
The edge of the board.

Rocker
The curve on the bottom of the board, from the nose to the tail, increases maneuverability, but decreases speed.

Fin
Fins are attached near the back of the board, which help keep the board from sliding sideways on the wave.

Tail
The back of the board.

Along with his accomplishments in board design, Blake is remembered for writing and surf photography. His first book, *Blake's Hawaiian Surfboard* (1931), had sections on the history of surfing, wave-riding techniques, and board construction. He also wrote articles on surfboard construction for *Popular Mechanics* and *Popular Science*. His surfing photos appeared in several publications, including *National Geographic*.

The earliest surfing competitions occurred in Hawaii where native chiefs competed for prizes of goods or livestock. The winner would usually be the surfer who had the longest ride or the first one to ride a wave to a designated point. When surfing enjoyed a resurgence in the early 1900s, so did surfing contests.

Still, it wasn't until the 1950s that competitive surfing received acceptance as a legitimate sport. In 1954, the Makaha International Surfing Championships were held for the first time, and until the early 1960s, they were regarded as the unofficial world championship.

The first World Surfing Championships were held in Sydney, Australia in 1964. One year later, the Tom Morey Invitational became the first competition to offer cash prizes. From 1961 to 1967, the United States Surfing Association (USSA) became a governing body for surfing competitions. After its founding in 1982, the Association of Surfing Professionals (ASP) became the current governing body for the world professional surfing tour. Over the years, media coverage of surfing competitions has been sporadic. In the early 1960s the ABC-TV program *Wide World of Sports* gave it annual coverage. That ended because of disputes over how much money the network would pay for broadcast rights.

From the late 1960s to the mid-1970s there was a strong disagreement over whether cash prizes and commercialization was good or bad for the sport. Surfers favoring money events said that it would give surfing greater media exposure and credibility. Amateurs and purists saw it as selling out. Bill Hamilton, who was widely regarded as surfing's best stylist in the 1960s and 70s, said: "surfing should not fit into contests, and contests should not fit into surfing."

With the advent of cable television and the Internet, surfing news and competitions are reaching a worldwide audience and interest in the sport will continue to greatly expand. The use of Web casts has made it possible for surfing fans to watch contests on their home computers. Like the Beach Boys sang in their 1962 hit, "Surfin Safari": "I tell you surfings mighty wild. It's getting bigger every day from Hawaii to the shores of Peru."

Duke Kahanamoku

Born in 1890, when Hawaii was still a U.S. possession and not a state, Duke Kahanamoku grew up near Waikiki Beach where he learned to swim and surf. Kahanamoku's swimming

Waikiki Beach circa 1900 *(Library of Congress)*

prowess became evident in a 1911 amateur swim meet where he broke two world records and tied a third.

Kahanamoku was clocked at 55.4 seconds in the 100-yard freestyle. He had beaten the existing world record by 4.6 seconds. Then he also broke the world record for the 220-yard freestyle and tied the record in the 50-yard freestyle.

Although the meet was sanctioned by the Amateur Athletic Union (AAU) and was officiated over by five certified judges, the AAU refused to recognize Kahanamoku's new records. They couldn't believe the results. It wouldn't be until years later that they would finally recognize his record-breaking achievements.

Kahanamoku's local fans gave him a chance to prove himself by raising money so he could compete for a spot on the 1912 U.S. Olympic swim team. Kahanamoku easily qualified for the team and won a gold medal in the 100-meter freestyle. He also swam in the 1920 and 1924 Olympics. Throughout his career, Kahanamoku won three gold medals and two silver medals.

Following his success in the Olympics, Kahanamoku began accepting invitations to give exhibitions at swim meets in the United States and other countries. During

Opening-day ceremony for the 1912 Summer Olympics in Stockholm, Sweden

these performances, Kahanamoku would demonstrate surfing as well as swimming. It was these surfing exhibitions that helped spread the sport's popularity throughout the United States.

One of Kahanamoku's most famous rides occurred in 1917 off the coast of Japan. The aftermath of an earthquake created a gigantic wave. While other beachgoers were running for shelter, Kahanamoku paddled out on his board. He rode the giant wave for more than a mile while it cut across several beaches.

"I didn't know that I was at the beginning of a ride that would become a celebrated and memoried thing," Kahanamoku recalled. "All I knew was that I had come to grips with the tallest, bulkiest, fastest wave I had ever seen."

Kahanamoku also showed that a surfboard could be used as a lifesaving device. In 1925, he rescued eight fisherman after their vessel capsized in heavy surf outside of Newport Beach, California. He used his surfboard to make quick trips back and forth from the ship to the shore.

When he wasn't riding the waves, Kahanamoku dabbled in movies and politics. From 1925 to 1967 he appeared in at least fifteen movies. His immense popularity with his fellow Hawaiians got him elected as sheriff of Honolulu thirteen consecutive times from 1932 to 1961.

Kahanamoku received many honors and accolades in his lifetime, including an induction into the Swimming Hall of Fame, the Surfing Hall of Fame, and the U.S. Olympic Hall of Fame. Thirty-one years after his death in 1968,

Kahamoku was named by *Surfer Magazine* as the most influential surfer of the twentieth century. In 2002, the United States Postal Service issued a commemorative stamp honoring the famous surfer.

Despite his many achievements and accomplishments, Kahanamoku was never known to be boastful. He once summed up his life and lasting influence by simply saying: "My boys and I, we showed the world how to go surfing."

three

Pro Circuit

When Kelly Slater became a full-time pro in 1991, he believed that he was good enough to compete with the best that the sport had to offer. The belief was based on a quiet self-assurance and not on a conceited cockiness. His only apparent doubt was if his style of surfing would be something the judges would be ready for.

In his opinion, the tendency of some current pro surfers to play it safe in crucial heats had made the sport boring. Instead of trying to dazzle the judges with new, creative acrobatic moves, the surfers stuck to their accustomed and predictable style. The style was powerful and smooth, but unexciting to Slater.

"I knew I was ready for the tour," Slater said. "But I didn't know if the tour was ready for me . . . The brand of surfing my friends and I were doing was an extreme change from what was going on at the time, and we didn't know if the judges would like it—but it wasn't going to stop us from trying."

Slater was part of an emerging group of surfers who took risks during competitions instead of playing it safe. *(Courtesy of Dan Merkel/A-Frame)*

Slater's first year as a pro was a learning experience. He competed in eleven Association of Surfing Professionals (ASP) events and never finished higher than fifth place. In four events, he wasn't even among the top forty surfers. At the end of the 1991 season, his ASP final ranking was a humbling forty-third place.

Bells Beach, Australia

Slater was unfazed by his disappointing rookie season. After all, he was only nineteen and it was his first year on the ASP World Championship Tour. The Rip Curl Classic at Bells Beach, Australia was the first ASP event in the 1992 season. Slater entered the event with dreams of being handed the winner's trophy. He was no longer a rookie, and he was confident that he'd get off to a good start.

Slater would later call his first 1992 competition "a rude awakening." He finished in thirtieth place, out of forty-eight surfers. Still, he wasn't discouraged. Even thirtieth was a step up from the year before.

The Association of Surfing Professionals

When Kelly Slater turned pro in 1990, the Association of Surfing Professionals (ASP) was the governing body of the world professional surfing tour. Its series of well organized competitions determine an annual men and women's champion and have done much to give the sport credibility and publicity.

Prior to the ASP's founding in 1982, the International Professional Surfers (IPS) created the pro circuit of tournaments that determined a world champion. The IPS was founded in 1976 by two former world champions—Fred Hemmings and Randy Rarick. Before then, surfers competed for prize money in an informal circuit of pro contests held in South Africa, Australia, and Hawaii, informally known as the "gypsy tour."

Initially, the IPS rated surfers by the amount of prize money they won in a year. Their first champion, South African surfer Shaun Thompson, won slightly more than $10,000 and their fifteenth ranked surfer made only $25 in one year.

Rarick and some other pro surfers convinced Hemmings to change the rankings system. The IPS switched to the format that's used by the ASP today. Surfers earn a number of points per event depending on how they place. The surfer scoring the most points in the series of sanctioned events becomes the world champion.

In 1976, Australian surfer Peter Townend became the IPS's first World Pro Tour

Champion. One year later, the IPS added a women's division and Hawaiian surfer Margo Oberg became its first champion. She also won the IPS's women's division in 1980 and 1981.

The IPS is credited with introducing head-to-head competition with one-on-one heats replacing the old format where as many as eight surfers would be competing on the same wave. It's also credited for adding California sites to the world tour schedule.

From 1976 to 1982 the prize money for IPS events increased from $77,650 to $338,100 for the men. The women's purses also showed a steady increase during those years, growing from $19,500 to $42,000. But a significant number of pro surfers felt that the organization wasn't growing fast enough. By the end of 1982, the ASP had taken its place.

The ASP has progressed slowly and steadily, but it has experienced some growing pains along the way. Its grueling circuit of up to twenty-five events in a season in the 1980s and the early 1990s led to three-time world champion Tom Curren dropping out of their tour. Several other top-rated surfers followed his lead.

The organization also hurt itself by continuing to hold events in South Africa in the 1980s when most other sports organizations were boycotting the country because of its policy of apartheid.

In the 1990s the ASP made some needed changes by scaling back on the number of events per season and adding more big wave sites to its schedule. Most recently it has expanded by adding new divisions for longboard, masters (thirty-six years old and over) and juniors (nineteen years old and under) competition.

"With so much pressure to start strong, someone else in my position might have been heartbroken, but I wasn't. It was thirteen places higher than I had finished the previous year, so I was stoked."

In his next four ASP events, Slater had two second-place and one third-place finish. He had yet to win a tourney, but he had moved into first place in the point totals that determine the world championship.

Slater celebrates his first-place finish at the 1992 Rip Curl Pro. *(Courtesy of Joli/A-Frame)*

Slater's first win in a World Tour Event occurred at the Rip Curl Pro in August 1992. The victory paid him $14,000 and solidified his lead in the point standings. By October 1992, though, he was feeling the pressure of being the points leader. He was only twenty years old, and the burden of being the best so early in his career caused him to change his strategy.

Slater speaks at a ceremony in 1992 where he accepted his first world championship title. *(Courtesy of Joli/A-Frame)*

"For the first time, I felt I would be letting people down if I failed to win the world title," Slater said. "I went from playing offense to playing defense. I had something to protect. With four events remaining, all I had to do was not screw up to win. It's difficult to surf freely when you're thinking like that."

A second-place finish at the Miyazaki Pro event in Japan gave Slater enough points to virtually ensure his first world championship. All he had to do to win the title was make a respectable showing at the Alternativa Surf International competition in Brazil. His ninth-place finish there was enough, and just two years after turning pro, Slater had won pro surfing's most prestigious title.

"When it came, I didn't know how to react," Slater admitted. "At age twenty, I was the youngest men's champ in history. I wanted to celebrate, but I felt that I was too young to have already reached the pinnacle of the sport. . . . I couldn't believe that I had won the world title ahead of my heroes—Tom Carroll, Tom Curren, and Martin Potter."

For Slater, winning the world title was a fantasy fulfilled. It validated his career choice and affirmed his enormous talent, but he admitted that it didn't make him any happier.

Shortly after becoming surfing's new world champion, he had another humbling experience. His manager contacted General Mills about getting Slater's face on a box of Wheaties. They rebuffed him by telling him that they only put "genuine athletes" on their cereal boxes. "To them, I was just a beach bum," Slater said.

Slater should have focused on defending his title, but the sudden fame and the opportunities that came with it proved to be a distraction.

Slater's agent, Brian Taylor, had told Slater that he was working on getting him on a TV show. Slater wasn't expecting that to happen, but decided to follow his manager's advice, and audition: even if he was cast, he could turn it down. He auditioned for a part on the show *Baywatch*, a popular syndicated series about lifeguards. Slater tried for the role of Jimmy Slade, a young surfer; he didn't expect to get the part. He would later learn that the part was written exclusively for him, and in April of 1992, Slater began appearing on *Baywatch*. At the height of its popularity, *Baywatch* was broadcast into more than 140 countries. It had an estimated worldwide audience of more than 1 billion viewers.

> Being on the show was something that I did against my better judgment. I was naïve to the bigger picture, but my manager, Bryan, and my mom thought it would be a great boost for my career. It happened so quickly that I didn't have time to stop it.

Although the show made Slater a celebrity, he didn't want fame. Worse, the show led to backlash from his fellow surfers. Many of them felt that Slater was selling out the sport. Slater was soon looking for a way to get out of the show. After he appeared in ten episodes, Slater's character was written out of the show. The writers had Jimmy Slade killed while trying to rescue his girlfriend from a kidnapper.

"I never thought that getting shot could feel so good," Slater joked. "It was too late to undo the damage acting on such a corny show had done to my image and to surfing, but at least it was over."

There was one positive result from Slater's brief time on *Baywatch*. He met actress and former

Playboy centerfold Pamela Anderson. After he left the show, they would enjoy an on-again, off-again relationship.

But even after leaving *Baywatch*, Slater found it difficult to regain his focus and concentrate on pro surfing. He was besieged with other issues. Only twenty-one himself, he had become engaged to seventeen-year-old Bree Pontoro. Soon, she was pressuring him to buy a house for them and set a wedding date.

Slater thought that he could please his fiancé by agreeing to buy a house. When he called his bank to get the money for a down payment, they told him that his account was overdrawn. It was a huge shock to discover that he had been spending money faster than he had been making it.

"I had made more than a million dollars and I had nothing to show for it," Slater recalled. "My mother and I were awful at managing money and we were unknowingly spending more than I was making. My manager asked me where the money was going, and I had no idea."

The Coke Classic in Sydney, Australia was the second event of the ASP's 1993 World Championship

Slater's Influence on Pop Culture

Though Kelly Slater was embarrassed by his stint on *Baywatch* and was eager to leave the show, he was not done appearing in pop culture. Though he largely stayed away from playing a fictional character as he did on *Baywatch*, Slater has appeared in a number of other films and television shows.

Most frequently, Slater turns up in various documentaries about the world of surfing. He appeared in *The Endless Summer 2*, the sequel to the famous 1966 surfing documentary. Both films were directed by Bruce Brown, a well-known documentarian who made numerous surfing films throughout his career, helping to bring greater national exposure to the sport. Additionally, Slater hosted *H3O*, a 1995-1998 television series about surfers and outdoor adventurers.

In 2003, Slater appeared in *Step Into Liquid*, a surfing documentary directed by Dana Brown, the son of Bruce Brown. The film delved into the world of Slater's generation of surfers, following them around the world to distant locations such as Ireland, Vietnam, and Rapa Nui. The film was well-received by critics, audiences, and the surfing community.

Slater did make some appearances in non-documentary films as well. In addition to a cameo role in the 2001 dark comedy *One Night at McCool's*, Slater appeared as himself and performed surfing stunts in 2004's *The Big Bounce*, a crime thriller set in Hawaii. Slater lent his voice to the 2007 animated comedy *Surf's Up*, about surfing penguins. Slater was joined by surfer Rob Machado in small roles as penguin versions of themselves.

Slater also busies himself in the world of music. An accomplished guitarist, he formed a band in the 1990s called The Surfers, who released an album of surf rock entitled *Songs From The Pipe*. He also contributed the original song "Never" to the soundtrack of the 1998 film *In God's Hands*.

Slater has appeared onstage with musicians Ben Harper and Eddie Vedder of Pearl Jam, and appeared in the 1999 music video for the song "You Look So Fine" by the band Garbage. Slater is good friends with the songwriter/surfer Jack Johnson, appearing in the surfing and music documentary *A Brokedown Melody*, which was soundtracked by Johnson's songs.

Slater has lent his voice and image to the world of video games. He appeared in *Tony Hawk's Pro Skater 3* in 2001, and in 2002 he had his own video game, *Kelly Slater's Pro Surfer*.

Finally, though Slater's affair with Pamela Anderson is his most well-known celebrity relationship, he has dated many other famous faces as well. He briefly dated Brazilian model Gisele Bündchen, and was spotted with actress Cameron Diaz. He has also been dating Israeli model Bar Rafaeli, with whom he traveled to Israel. During one trip he was detained by police after trying to stop paparazzi from photographing him and Rafaeli.

Tour. It would be the worst performance in Slater's pro career. He finished in last place; Slater began having major doubts about his skills, and he began losing his zest for competing.

"I had no confidence in my surfing, my boards, or competition skills," Slater admitted. "I started to believe that my world title was a fluke."

But Slater was too competitive and too analytical to keep on losing. He turned things around by collecting the judge's score sheets and studying them to see what was costing him points. He began pinpointing his mistakes and working to correct them. Slater also began paying more attention to the conditions and patiently waiting for the best waves.

Another major factor in Slater's turnaround was his willingness to ask for help. Even though he was the reigning world champion, he wasn't too proud to ask for advice and coaching. Two-time world champion Tom Carroll became one of Slater's major mentors.

"He was sort of my big brother on tour and helped get me focused on surfing again," Slater said.

Even though his focus and enthusiasm had returned, Slater's comeback was a gradual process. He had another last-place finish before closing out the season with four good performances in WCT events. He won the Marui Pro event in Japan and

Slater surfing at Huntington Beach, California, in 1994 *(Courtesy of Jeff Gross/Allsport/Getty Images)*

placed second in the Chiemsee Pipe Masters in Japan, finishing the year ranked seventh in the world.

By February 1994, Slater had totally rededicated himself to pro surfing. He was starting to get his finances in order and he had broken off his engagement with Bree. The breakup was difficult, but he had surfing to fill the emotional void in his life.

"I redirected my emotions into surfing," Slater said. "My only focus became refining my skills and becoming a better competitor. I was determined to win everything in sight. Surfing was my savior, and competition was the ultimate escape."

four

New School, New Life

By 1994, the veteran surfers who had dominated the pro surfing circuit had been labeled the Old School; Slater and the other up-and-coming surfers had been labeled the New School. While Slater had tried to incorporate both styles in his performance, he couldn't avoid being labeled New School. "As much as I hoped that my approach was a good mix of the two styles, the surfing media as well as the older guys on the tour went out of their way to label me as a New Schooler," he said.

Slater kicked off the 1994 ASP World Tour by winning the Rip Curl Pro at Bells Beach, Australia.

Slater celebrates his 1994 Rip Curl Pro win at Bells Beach, Australia.
(Courtesy of Joli/A-Frame)

The win not only showed surfing fans that Slater was back and stronger than ever, it showed that the New School was ready to take over.

The next ASP event after Bell's was the Marui Pro in Japan. Slater finished in third place, but he wasn't upset at not winning. He was delighted because the tournament was won by Rob Machado, another New School surfer. Machado dominated the event by surfing faster in small waves. To the judges, speed was becoming more important than power.

The sudden rise to dominance of the New School greatly vindicated Slater. "It finally felt like I was part of a group, rather than an outsider among the Old Schoolers." he explained. "As each new kid made his mark, we fed off of the other's success. If I lost a contest, I'd pull for my friends to win."

Slater finished out 1994 with six wins and five second-place finishes in twenty-one events. He easily won his second ASP World Championship Tour title along with the World Qualifying Series. His dominance in the pro events boosted his popularity among surfing fans. For the first time, he won *Surfer Magazine*'s annual Surfer Poll popularity contest.

But his success wasn't making him popular with some of his competitors. Barton Lynch, a former world champion surfer, worried Slater was holding other surfers back.

"During our era, roughly 1983 to 1993, there were a lot of guys with the potential to win. When Slater came along, there were great surfers, but none of them were able to live up to their potential because of his dominance."

At the same time that Slater was beginning to dominate pro surfing, Pamela Anderson unexpectedly reentered his life. Slater claimed that he had not been attracted to her while they were appearing on *Baywatch*, but in late 1994, he saw her in Hawaii while she was making a TV special. They began dating, but Slater found that they had different priorities and expectations. Anderson, five years older than Slater, was ready to settle down, but married life and a family held no interest for twenty-two-year-old Slater.

Even though Slater felt that he wasn't ready to start a family, he unexpectedly became a father. In the summer of 1995, Slater had briefly dated a woman named Tamara. She lived in Fort Lauderdale, Florida.

Slater and Pamela Anderson *(Courtesy of Rupert Thorpe/Getty Images)*

In October 1995, she drove to Slater's condo in Cocoa Beach and told him that she was pregnant.

Tamara told Slater that she was going to have their child, even if he didn't want to get involved in the child's life. Slater called that choice A. Choice B was trying to renew their relationship and being a couple again. A third option was for them to remain apart and for them to be single parents sharing in the child rearing.

Slater decided that choices A and B weren't feasible. He wanted to be involved in raising the child, but he was firmly convinced that their relationship was definitely over. He told Tamara that he wanted to be involved in their child's life. Then he thought about how his life would be changing.

"I was still a kid myself. Until that day, I had one responsibility, which was to win surf contests. I'd never had a real job or paid a bill, but it was time to grow up. Things were different now. I was going to be a father."

In spite of the distractions of impending fatherhood, Slater won his second consecutive world championship in 1995. His primary competition

Slater poses with his trophy after winning the 1995 world championship.
(Courtesy of Joli/A-Frame)

Rob Machado *(Courtesy of Getty Images)*

that year was his friend and fellow surfer Rob Machado, and they pushed each other to surf with more conviction and energy than ever before. Slater even considered "the 1995 title heat with Rob . . . the best heat of my life."

Despite being beaten, Machado also viewed the 1995 competition fondly:

> It's still really fresh in my mind. Like it happened yesterday. Those moments don't come along very often. It's actually become even better over the years, just because we've had time to talk about it. To reflect on it, and really kind of analyze it, and be like: wow that was crazy . . . Some people say that I should have ran him over, and try to win the world title. But I look back, and have been like "Well I would have been a totally different person." It would have changed my course a little. I'm glad it ended up the way it did.

But despite his success and satisfaction, at the age of twenty-three, he was starting to feel as if there was nothing left to accomplish.

"I had achieved all I wanted from surfing. Since I had taken better care of my money, I had all that I'd ever need. There was no way I could get so much satisfaction from a surf contest again. It almost seemed a waste of time to try."

Although he kept it to himself, Slater found a new goal to keep him motivated. From 1979 to 1982, Mark Richards had won four consecutive world titles. Slater had won three world titles in four years. Breaking Richards's record became Slater's next goal.

"I kept going because I wanted to try to match Mark Richards's record of four world titles. At the same time, I was thinking ahead to a fifth title, because that would tie Mark's record of four in a row. But nobody wants to just tie a record; I'd have to go for six. It wasn't cockiness, but I needed to set high goals to stay focused."

Slater's relentless pursuit of setting new records was temporarily halted when his daughter, Taylor, was born on June 4, 1996. He had just finished competing in a surf meet in Indonesia, and spent the next two days traveling to Florida see his newborn child. Since then, he's remained involved in Taylor's life. Still, he acknowledges that surfing stardom has often caused him to be an absentee father.

Along with a private life that was becoming stressful and complicated, Slater's professional life wasn't exactly a smooth riding wave. Although he won his third consecutive world championship in 1996, the title was shrouded in controversy.

That year, Slater had been chasing Shane Beschen. Slater and Shane had a friendly rivalry that preceded

Shane Beschen *(Getty Images)*

their pro careers. In 1985, Slater had defeated Shane in the Boy's Division of the U.S. Surfing Championships. About halfway through the season, Shane had a big lead in points. But prior to the U.S. Open in Huntington Beach, California, Slater had closed the gap by winning his last two competitions.

A win at the U.S. Open would keep it close. A poor showing would probably torpedo Slater's chances of winning his third straight world title.

The final heat of the event was a showdown between Slater and Shane. They paddled out to catch the same wave. Neither surfer had priority for riding it, but according to the rules, the surfer closest to the wave's curl has the right of way. Slater was the closest to the curl, so Shane was penalized for interference. That caused the judges to give Shane a zero score for that ride.

The interference call enabled Slater to place second in the U.S. Open. He followed that up with back-to-back, first-place finishes at a couple of ASP WCT events in France, giving him enough points to clinch his third straight world title with one event left.

In 1997, Slater had a sensational season. He won five of the first six ASP WCT events that year. That gave him such a big point lead that he was able to ease up in the second half of the season. He easily won a fourth consecutive world title, tying Mark Richards's record.

During his pro career, Slater had always been analytical about his performance and technique. But this time, he became obsessive about analyzing and improving his surfing skills. He paid more attention to elements like weight distribution and how it applied to the curve of the wave. Slater began noting if his speed increased or decreased when he came out of a turn, and he discovered how to find the perfect spot to ride a wave that would allow him the ultimate amount of freedom and versatility to do tricks and ride successfully.

As the 1998 ASP World Tour approached, Slater was positioned to become the first surfer to win five consecutive world titles. Yet, he was having problems; he felt so pressured his hair began falling out. Slater shaved his head and began wondering how much longer he could endure the annual pro tour. His motivation to compete, worn down by years of living his life in the public eye and constantly struggling to top himself, was gone.

Regardless, the 1998 season started off well with Slater winning the first APS WCT event, the Billabong Pro in Australia. But in the next five events, Slater had three fifth-place finishes and two seventeenth-place finishes. That dropped him to fifth in the point standings, his lowest ranking since 1993.

After a fifth-place finish at the Op Pro in Huntington Beach, California, Slater felt like there was a tug-of-war between his desire to win a record-breaking six straight world titles and his desire to just go out and have fun surfing.

"Because I had used surfing to escape my emotions, I had built up a wall that had separated me from my family and friends. . . . I wanted to achieve my ultimate mission of six world titles, but not by sacrificing everything else. Win or lose, I wanted to enjoy the ride."

Huntington Beach, California

The Pipeline Masters in Hawaii was the final 1998 ASP WCT event. Slater had won the event three years in a row (1994–1996), so he should been have been brimming with confidence. Instead, he was plagued by anxiety and doubts. After advancing through the first two rounds, Slater again had to face Rob Machado. A win in that heat would guarantee his fifth consecutive world title.

"Here was my chance. My season, my career, and my legacy would all be decided in a twenty-five minute session with Rob Machado. I could seize the opportunity or buckle under the pressure, and I felt myself buckling."

Slater's friend, Tom Carroll, saw how stressed and nervous Slater was. He had been with him when Slater won his first world title in 1992, and throughout Slater's career, Tom had helped him get through tense, high-pressure situations. He relaxed Slater by putting him through some relaxing yoga poses.

Slater credits Rob with pushing him on to an exceptional performance. Slater won the heat and broke Mark Richards's incredible record.

Mark Richards graciously congratulated Slater. He wasn't jealous or resentful that someone from the

New School had broken his record. He told Slater: "If I had to see it fall, I'm stoked to see it be to a guy who has changed our perception of what high-performance competitive surfing is. I'd hate to see it go to someone who managed to win a billion contests by riding four waves to the beach rather than a guy who pushed the boundaries."

Amid all the celebrating and hoopla, Slater saw his daughter, Taylor, playing on the beach. Tamara had surprised him by bringing her to Hawaii. He was thrilled that she was there: "One of the best things about this world title was that she was a part of it," he said.

He walked over to her and saw that she was unimpressed by his mob of fans. She looked at her father and asked him to build sand castles with her. Slater decided then that winning a sixth consecutive world title was no longer important. He explained:

> [Taylor] just knows me as Daddy, not as some surfer guy. She didn't have any idea that something special was going on, that she was at some contest that I had to do good in. So I won the title and came out of the water, everybody's freaking out, and my daughter's

playing in the sand, minding her own business. She's not even aware . . . everyone's screaming for me, yelling, and she's sitting there, telling people to be quiet. She's like, "Shhhhh, be quiet!" She's pissed off at everyone 'cause they wouldn't shut up. It was like a dose of reality splashed into this moment of glory—a little window into the future.

The next evening, Slater announced that he was retiring from pro surfing. It wouldn't be full-time retirement. He would still compete in selected events, but pro surfing would no longer be his top priority. Slater's life and career would be entering a new phase.

five

Back to the Waves

A self-imposed retirement gave Slater time to pause and reflect on his life. He had been tremendously successful, but success always came at a price. For Slater, the price had been not getting to know himself, his family, and his friends.

"For most of my life, I derived my self-worth from how well I rode my surfboard," Slater said. "I thought that the better I did, the more people would like me. Obviously, that wasn't the case. I had lots of fans, but that's superficial. . . . There had to be more to life than trying to adhere to others' criteria of how they think I should ride a wave."

Quicksilver, the world's largest manufacturer of surf apparel and accessories, had been Slater's major sponsor during his pro career. Whenever Slater wanted to compete in an event, they would send him there. They were still paying him for endorsing their products, so Slater was free of any money worries.

But even with a reduced schedule of competitive surfing events, Slater wasn't going to let his skills erode. He was still too much of a competitor to completely give it up. He set a personal goal of winning one WCT event each year in order to keep himself from getting too complacent or letting his abilities erode.

In 1999, Slater realized that goal by the Pipeline Masters. He surfed in three other ASP WCT events that year, but didn't concern himself with amassing points or chasing a championship.

Along with pro surfing, there was something else that Slater couldn't completely give up during his retirement—having Pamela Anderson in his life.

They started dating again in 1998 and continued their on-and-off relationship until 2000. When they renewed their relationship, Pamela had recently

Slater started dating Pamela Anderson again in 1998. Here, they sit together during a Lakers basketball game in 2000. *(Courtesy of Joe Thomas/ Getty Images)*

divorced her rock star husband, Tommy Lee. Slater wanted their relationship to be free from large-scale media coverage, but Pamela was such a huge celebrity that was impossible.

"I became more famous for dating her than for anything that I had achieved in surfing. I was in the gossip magazines every week," Slater recalled.

Pamela briefly reconciled with Tommy Lee, but in early 2000 she began dating Slater again. Slater later said that taking another chance at establishing a relationship with her was against his better judgment. Finally, he realized that it wasn't going to work. Even after knowing each other for many years, Slater and Anderson's lives remained too different, and their priorities too far apart.

In his second year of retirement, Slater limited himself to five events. He won the first event he entered, the ASP WCT Gotcha Pro Tahiti, and coasted through the other four. He was winning less but enjoying it more. Without the pressure or worrying about winning heats or scoring points, Slater was able to take chances.

"I was free to experiment for the first time in my life," he said. "I wanted to see if the moves that I had imagined as a kid were possible."

He enjoyed trying to copy some of the spins and flips that he had seen skateboarders perform. In the 1999 Pipe Masters, he tried a flip after twisting 540 degrees. A missed landing kept him from pulling it off.

"It's a lot harder to control and land a six-foot surfboard than a two-and-a-half foot skateboard,"

Slater surfing in the 2000 Pipe Masters. During his self-imposed retirement, Slater competed in several events each year to keep his skills intact. (*Courtesy of Pierre Tostee/Allsport*)

Slater explained. "Plus the wave is a moving target as opposed to a ramp or sidewalk."

In 2000 and 2001, Slater only competed in ten events. He still realized his goal of winning one event each year, though: the first year, the win came at the Gotcha Pro Tahiti, and the following year, he won the Quicksilver King of the Peak in Sebastian

Inlet, Florida. The reduced schedule gave Slater more free time to spend with his family, particularly his father.

In October 2000, Slater learned that his father, Steve, had throat cancer. Even though Slater hadn't had a close relationship with his dad, he felt a need to be with him. He also felt an obligation to pay for Steve's medical bills. The treatment involved some expensive experimental drugs that weren't covered by health insurance.

At first, Steve refused to allow his son to pay. But Slater persisted and Steve gave in. "With all the money I had made throughout the years, my dad never asked me for a dime," Slater said. "He didn't even want to ask when his life depended on it. . . . His selflessness showed me a lot about his character."

But the experimental drugs and expensive treatments weren't able to keep Steve from succumbing to cancer; he died in 2002. After years of estrangement, though, Slater and his father were able to rebuild their bond. Slater said that when Steve died, he did it without complaining or bemoaning his fate, and Slater too was able

Slater has expressed that he would like to work with the Sea Shepherd Conservation Society.

to accept his father's death without any regrets or guilt.

Slater also used his time away from surfing to learn about environmental issues, a cause he continues to be involved in today. In an interview with the *Los Angeles Times*, Slater said that he would like to work with the Sea Shepherd Conservation Society and its leader, Paul Watson. Watson and his organization have been confronting fisherman for illegally harvesting whales and dolphins, leading to the arrests of poachers and saving marine life.

"[Paul Watson] almost single-handedly saved tens of thousands of whales and probably hundreds of thousands of dolphins around the world," Slater told reporter Pete Thomas. "He's been busting people and they can do some pretty radical things at sea

The Sea Shepherd Conservation Society works to save dolphins and whales from poachers.

where, if you're doing something illegally, it's kind of open game on your boat."

Slater has also shown his commitment to the environment by partnering with an organization known as Carbonfund. Carbon emissions from gas and other fossil fuels have been cited as the chief culprit in causing global warming. Carbonfund calculates how much each person contributes in carbon emissions from driving, flying, and energy consumption. Then they give the person different options—such as planting trees—that would offset the emissions they've created.

Slater calculated that he's flown and driven more than 4 million miles to compete in surfing events. He's tried to offset that by paying for five acres of trees to be replanted near a beach in Nicaragua. He says that his ultimate goal is to get all the surfers in the ASP World Tour to join in.

"There are many people out there unconvinced as to our effect on the world's climate," Slater admits. "I have to admit at time I wonder what the exact science is. But here's the clincher for me: if you plant more trees and use more land for good you will have better air quality. Simple as that."

Planting trees in Nicaragua is another way Slater contributes to conservation.

Regardless of the various ways he busied himself, Slater couldn't fully turn his back on competitive surfing. "I could take myself out of competition, but I couldn't get the competitiveness out of me," he said. In October 2001 he issued a press release saying that he would return and pursue his seventh world title in 2002.

Slater smiles at fellow surfer Sunny Garcia (right) during a press conference held to announce Slater's return to professional surfing.

While Slater was as competitive as ever, the effects of a three-year layoff from full-time surfing were showing. In 2002, he competed in ten ASP events and won one. He finished the year with ASP WCT tour final ranking of ninth place.

That year, Slater began an increasingly intense rivalry with Andy Irons. Irons was six years younger than Slater, brash, and wasn't afraid to publicly disrespect Slater.

In 2003, *Surfing* magazine described Irons' skills: "He has the miraculous combination of big-wave

Andy Irons *(Courtesy of Karen Wilson/ASP/Getty Images)*

craziness and small wave ripping down better than any surfer in the world right now."

In 2003, Slater continued his comeback by moving up to a number two ranking, but he watched Irons win a second consecutive world title. The following year, Slater fell to third while Irons notched his third straight world championship.

By then, their rivalry was at its zenith, and Slater prepared to face Irons at the XBOX Pipeline Masters, an event held at Oahu Beach in Hawaii where the waves break a mere seventy-five yards off of the beach. They break with such force that at least a dozen surfers have died there over the years.

Because of the uniqueness of the waves at Oahu Beach, surfers call the event a tube-riding contest. The tube is the hollow area of the wave. According to *The Encyclopedia of Surfing*, less than 5 percent of the world's surfers have the skill to consistently get inside the tube and most tube rides last for less than three seconds. The winner of the XBOX Pipeline Masters is usually the surfer who can ride deepest in the tube for the longest time and do it more consistently than his opponents.

If Slater won the event, he would clinch an unprecedented seventh world championship. The final heat came down to a showdown between Slater and Irons. Their rivalry was intense; at least one account claims that Irons tried to unhinge Slater by screaming vulgarities at him, and that Slater infuriated Irons by patronizingly telling him to calm down.

Both surfers did their best, but the judges considered Irons to be the better surfer. Irons became the first surfer to beat Slater in a one-on-one showdown, winning the championship in the process.

After the competition was over, Irons challenged Slater to face him again. He slapped Slater on the back and said: "It's on. See you next year."

That was all the challenge and motivation that Slater needed. Slater geared up to reclaim the championship in 2005, and during the next few months, the intense rivals traded contest wins, but by October 2005, Slater had more points than his rival. If Slater could win at the Nova Schin Surf Festival in Brazil, he would be crowned the 2005 world champion. If he lost, his only chance would be to beat Irons at the Pipeline competition, where Slater hadn't won since 1999.

Perhaps due to the pressure, Slater didn't perform well at Nova Schin; he lost in the quarterfinals to a relative unknown. Fortunately for Slater, though, Irons was also having an off day. Irons did so badly that Slater's point lead held up—Slater had defeated his rival and won his seventh world championship.

"This was probably my most complete win," Slater told a writer from *Transworld Surf* magazine. "I feel like I'm bringing the pieces of my life together. That's what [this world championship] symbolized to me."

The win showed unequivocally that Slater was a master surfer, and Irons was still just an upstart. Journalist Daniel Duane pointed out: "Raised on videos of Slater, Irons has always been a brilliant student of his surfing style. But the one thing that Irons hasn't absorbed is the relentless consistency and strategic focus that make Slater so good at winning contests."

Still, Slater's 2005 win wasn't the end of pro surfing's most watched and publicized rivalry. In June

Slater celebrates winning his seventh world title. *(Courtesy of Karen Wilson/ASP/Getty Images)*

2006, Irons beat Slater in a competition in Mexico. Once again, he told Slater: "That's it, Game On!"

Still, Slater won the 2006 season overall, snagging an incredible eighth world championship. According to Rob Machado, the win wasn't a surprise, as Slater was as strong a surfer as ever. "He's a freak," Machado said. "He's always been a freak. We've always looked at him like that. When he really wants to do something, and he's focused . . . The guy is really hard to beat. He's an amazing surfer."

After the win, Slater was proud but was unsure whether or not he'd seek a ninth title. "I feel like I'm surfing as strong and as good as ever," he said. "I feel like I'm competing better than ever. It makes me feel like I can keep going if I want. I just don't know if that's what I want now."

However, in 2007, Slater returned to defend his title. He set yet another record by winning his thirty-fourth ASP WCT event. Tom Curren had been the previous record holder with thirty-three. With three events left in the ASP WCT tour, Slater was in second place. Australian surfer Mick Fanning was enjoying a 1,020 point lead over Slater. Fanning's lead was large but not insurmountable. But even if

Fanning takes away Slater's title, Slater may get it back in the future. He's said that he could compete into his forties, and hasn't indicated any plans to retire soon.

Whether he wins or loses, Kelly Slater has made a significant mark on the surfing world. With an unprecedented number of wins, and a charisma that has helped spread his reputation and fame far beyond surfing fans, Slater has undoubtedly become one of surfing's most important figures. And even if he retires from competitive surfing, there's no doubt that Slater, who found his peace and purpose in the water, will ever give up riding the waves.

Timeline

1972   Born February 11, 1972, in Cocoa Beach, Florida.

1980   Wins first surfing competition in the eight and under division.

1984   Wins first U.S. Amateur Championship in the Menehune Division.

1986   Begins competing and winning in pro-am competitions.

1987– 1990   Continues to compete as an amateur while attending Cocoa Beach High School.

1990   Turns pro in July; surfs in seven professional tournaments, wins two.

1991	Graduates from Cocoa Beach High School in June; finishes first season on ASP World Championship Tour ranked forty-third.
1992– 1993	Wins first ASP World Championship at age twenty, the youngest surfer to win the title; plays a recurring role on TV show *Baywatch*; ends 1992 season ranked seventh.
1994– 1998	Wins ASP World Championship Tour five years in a row to become six-time world champion.
1999– 2001	Stops competing full time.
2002	Returns to competing on the ASP World Championship Tour full time; finishes season ranked ninth.

2005   Wins ASP World Championship for a record seventh time.

2006   Wins eighth ASP World Championship at age thirty-four, the oldest surfer to win the title.

2007   Wins his thirty-fourth ASP WCT event.

Sources

CHAPTER ONE:
Paddling Out

p. 11, "It was a great . . ." Kelly Slater with Jason Borte, *Pipe Dreams A Surfer's Journey* (New York: HC Publishers, 2003), 22.

p. 12, "I think that it . . ." Ibid., 23.

p. 13, "I wanted to surf . . ." Ibid., 26.

p. 14, "radical controlled maneuvers . . ." Daniel Duane, "When A Man Loves A Rival," *New York Times Magazine*, August 20, 2006.

p. 17, "It was the first . . ." Slater, *Pipe Dreams A Surfer's Journey*, 43.

p. 17, "Surfing was the one . . ." Ibid., 46.

p. 17-18, "I never could see . . ." Ibid., 48.

p. 19, "These experiences were just . . ." Ibid., 80.

p. 19, "Deep down, he was . . ." Ibid., 78.

p. 21, "As competitive as I . . ." Ibid., 93.

p. 21, "If you can't finish . . ." Ibid., 129.

CHAPTER TWO:
History of the Surf

p. 27-28, "In one place we . . ." Mark Twain, *Twainquotes.com*, http://www.twainquotes.com/ Surfing.html.

p. 40, "surfing should not fit . . ." Matt Warshaw, *The Encyclopedia of Surfing* (Orlando: Harcourt, Inc. 2003), 478.

p. 41, "I tell you surfings . . ." Brian Wilson, "Surfin Safari," *Pet Sounds*, http://www. lyricsfreak.com/b/beachboys/surfin + safari_ 20013993.html.

p. 44, "I didn't know . . ." Malcolm Gault-Williams, *Legendary Surfers* (CafePress print on-demand, 2005), http://www. hawaiianswimboat.com/duke4.html.

p. 45, "My boys and I . . . " Joe Doggett, "Like Hawaii's Surf, Memories Surge on a Return to Waikiki," *Houston Chronicle*, August 8, 1996.

CHAPTER THREE:
Pro Circuit

p. 47, "I knew I was ready . . ." Slater, *Pipe Dreams A Surfer's Journey*, 138.

p. 49, "a rude awakening" Ibid., 140.

p. 52, "With so much pressure . . ." Ibid., 141.

p. 55, "For the first time . . ." Ibid., 146.

p. 55, "when it came, . . ." Ibid., 149.

p. 56, "To them I was . . ." Ibid., 153.

p. 57, "Being on the show . . ." Ibid., 155-156.

p. 57, "I never thought that . . ." Ibid., 163.

p. 58, "I had made more . . ." Ibid., 166.

p. 62, "I had no confidence .." Ibid., 167.

p. 62, "He was sort of . . ." Ibid., 169.

p. 64, "I redirected my emotions . . ." Ibid., 173.

CHAPTER FOUR:
New School, New Life

p. 65, "As much as I . . ." Slater, *Pipe Dreams A Surfer's Journey*, 176.

p. 67, "It finally felt like . . ." Ibid., 177.

p. 67, "During our era . . ." Ibid., 187.

p. 70, "I was still a kid . . ." Ibid., 202-203.

p. 72, "The 1995 title heat . . ." "Kelly Slater: Lonely at the Top," *Irish Surf Base,* http://www.geocities.com/Pipeline/1597/kellyslater.html.

p. 73, "It's still really fresh . . ." Richard Livsey, "The Planet Reef Tour 2006: Rob Machado and Company Roll Into Long Island," *RichardLivsey.com,* http://www.richardlivsey.com/rob.html.

p. 73, "I had achieved all . . ." Slater, *Pipe Dreams A Surfer's Journey,* 217.

p. 74, "I kept going because . . ." Ibid.

p. 78, "Because I had used . . ." Ibid., 251.

p. 79, "Here was my chance . . ." Ibid., 255-256.

p. 80, "If I had to see . . ." Ibid., 257.

p. 80, "One of the best . . ." "Kelly Slater: Lonely at the Top."

p. 80-81, "[Taylor] just knows me . . ." Ibid.

CHAPTER FIVE:
Back to the Waves

p. 82, "For most of my life . . ." Slater, *Pipe Dreams A Surfer's Journey,* 261-262.

p. 87, "I became more famous for . . ." Ibid. 263.

p. 85, "I was free to experiment . . . " Ibid. 267.

p. 85-86, "It's a lot harder to control . . ." Ibid. 268.

p. 87, "With all the money . . ." Ibid. 283.

p. 89-90, "[Paul Watson] almost single-handedly . . ." Pete Thomas, "Wave of the future, Slater, nearing the end of his competitive surfing career, is planning to work with conservation society," *Los Angeles Times*, September 8, 2007.

p. 90, "There are many people . . ." Evan Slater, "Kelly Slater Goes Carbon Neutral," *Surfing Magazine*, www.surfingthemag.com.

p. 91, "I could take myself out . . ." Slater, *Pipe Dreams A Surfer's Journey*, 289.

p. 92-93, "He has the miraculous . . ." Warshaw, *The Encyclopedia of Surfing,* 294.

p. 95, "It's on . . . next year," Duane, "When A Man Loves a Rival."

p. 95 , "That was probably my . . ." Justin Tejada, "The Big Kahuna with Seven World Championships, Kelly Slater is the Best Surfer Ever," *Sports Illustrated for Kids*, April 1, 2006.

p. 96, "Raised on videos . . ." Ibid.

p. 97, "That's it. Game on!" Ibid.

p. 97, "He's a freak . . ." Livsey, "The Planet Reef Tour 2006."

p. 97, "I feel like I'm surfing . . ." "Kelly Slater claims record breaking 8th world surfing title," *Surfers Village*, www.surfersvillage.com.

Bibliography

Duane, Daniel. "When A Man Loves A Rival."
New York Times Magazine, August 20, 2006.

Hynd, Derek. "Long Live the King." *Surfer*,
Autumn 2001.

Kahn, Jordan. "Slater: No One Has Dominated."
Daytona Beach (Fl.) News-Journal, June 6,
2007.

Kampion, Drew. *The Way of the Surfer*. New
York: Harry N. Abrams, Inc. Publishers, 2003

"Kelly Slater claims record breaking 8th surfing."
Surfers Village. http://www.surfersvillage.com.

"Kelly Slater: Lonely at the Top." *Irish Surf Base*,
http://www.geocities.com/Pipeline/1597/
kellyslater.html.

Livsey, Richard. "The Planet Reef Tour 2006:
Rob Machado and Company Roll Into
Long Island." *RichardLivsey.com*. http://www.
richardlivsey.com/rob.html.

Lulham, Amanda. "Unstoppable Slater Claims
Wins Record." *Daily Telegraph,* (Sydney,
Australia), September 17, 2007.

Mauro, Chris. "The Hot Seat with Kelly Slater."
Surfer, October 2003.

Murphy, Austin. "Back on Board." *Sports
Illustrated,* February 18, 2002.

Slater, Evan. "Kelly Slater Goes Carbon Neutral."
Surfing Magazine, http://www.surfingthemag.
com.

Slater, Kelly. *Pipe Dreams: A Surfer's Journey*.
In collaboration with Jason Borte. New York:
Reagan Books, 2003.

"The *Surfer* Interview with Kelly Slater." *Surfer,*
February 2002.

Tejada, Justin. "The Big Kahuna With Seven
World Championships, Kelly Slater Is the Best
Surfer Ever." *Sports Illustrated for Kids,*
April 1, 2006.

Thomas, Pete. "Slater Is Making His Move."
Los Angeles Times, September 14, 2007.

_____. "Wave of the future; Slater nearing the end of his competitive surfing career, is planning to work with conservation society." *Los Angeles Times*, September 8, 2007.

Warshaw, Matt. *The Encyclopedia of Surfing*. Orlando: Harcourt Inc., 2003.

Web sites

http://www.aspworldtour.com
Along with the current point standings in the Association of Surfing Professionals (ASP) World Tour competition, this Web site has a history of the ASP as well as answers to frequently asked questions about the organization.

http://www.surfingthemag.com
Current articles about Kelly Slater and other surfers along with news about the latest events. Blogs, photos, and videos are also included.

http://www.surfline.com
Surf news, photos, Web cams and weather forecasts. Site also has information on surfing excursions and vacations.

Index